Better by Design
Your Best Collaboration Guide

Better by Design

Your Best Collaboration Guide

How to Produce Better Outcomes
through Well Designed Collaborations

David B. Savage

Contents

"The world has got more complex and more interconnected, and so has its challenges. The time of the lone wolf is over. Now we need to work together as never before, bringing together diverse groups of stakeholders to put ego aside and work co-creatively towards solutions. Effective collaboration is no longer a "nice to have" skill. It's crucial."

Roz Savage MBE
Author | Speaker | Ocean Rower
Guinness World Record Holder
Yale World Fellow

Why Buy and Use This Guide Book?

> "We can only meet our critical global and local challenges
> with collective intelligence."
>
> *Roz Savage, MBE*

Work is challenging. Volunteer work is challenging. Life is challenging. And getting more complex every week. Yet, we expect to be more productive and successful each day.

We know that we can achieve far more, far more effectively and efficiently when we work together well. But how do we do that? This book is your guide. Use it to:

1. Learn more about collaboration

2. Lead your teams

3. Generate, decide, design, assess, and complete your initiatives

This guide is your hands-on planner. I offer it to you so you can produce better outcomes. This is How To. And this book will become your ongoing reference.

Better by Design is the 7th in my *Break Through to Yes* series on collaboration.

2016: *Unlocking the Possible within a Culture of Collaboration*

2017: *The Foundations for Collaboration,*
The Collaborative Guests Podcasts,
The 10 Essential Steps to Collaboration, and
Unlocking the Possible with Collaboration

2018: *Unlocking the Possible within a Culture of Collaboration*
(revised and updated), and
Better by Design: Your Best Collaboration Guide

My previous books, co-authored, are *Ready Aim Excel: 52 Leadership Lessons* (2012) and *Let's Talk: A Company to Company Council Dispute Resolution Handbook* (2004). My *Sustain Magazine* (2013) served organizations committed to the economic and social opportunities of sustainability.

Why me? I will help you solve your challenges and capture your opportunities with my unique background and proven leadership in helping people and organizations work together better. I bring you:

1. Over 42 years of leadership, negotiation, collaboration, and dispute resolution,

2. Three decades of volunteering for, and in some cases leading, important not-for-profits organizations

3. Published seven books on collaboration, co-authored a book on leadership, and co-authored a book on dispute resolution between companies

4. Coached leaders for more than ten years

5. Hosted 45 podcasts on collaborative leadership

6. Developed a 360 assessment for organizational/team development

7. Surveyed leaders in several industries and not-for-profits, as well as Rotary International and the Heart and Stroke Foundation

I realize there is a significant gap. That gap is the absence of a readily accessible, informative, and practical guide for you. You may not have the time or resources to bring together all the wisdom. And you still have dreams, aspirations, purpose, and teams to create, encourage, and accomplish.

This *Better by Design* guide book is intended to help you decide, design, assess, lead, and succeed with your initiatives and projects. This book is intended to serve you and your organization. As you design and lead your next initiative, my vision is that you will minimize inefficiencies, maximize results, build stronger project teams, and change your world with the help of *Better by Design*. Use this guide over and over—as the fresh starting place for you to generate your own practical methods and energized visions.

> **"When you have a precise template for your project, only then may you be exceptionally creative."**
>
> *Glenn Dobie, Kootenay Rockies Gran Fondo and Cranbrook Sunrise Rotary*

Prologue

I've been asked many times why I have done this series. Why have I written seven *Break Through to Yes* books (print, eBook and Audio)? Why is collaboration so important?

I'll tell you why. We need it. I need it. Our future needs it. Business is forced into silos and must give up to an open and agile system that better suits today's world and our shared future. We must create shared value. We must think critically. The costs of command-and-control leadership are getting higher.

During my 42-year career in business, I've held titles including director, president, and chief operating officer. I have seen many and repeated failures, some of which cost billions. These failures affect organizations and their capital projects and operations. When a company starts making mistakes, tries to force its agenda on others, or conflicts with its own stakeholders, the consequences are significant. People revolt and profit margins are destroyed. Projects get delayed in regulatory and community review for extended lengths of time. Employees simply don't give their best because they do not trust the systems they work in especially when they have little influence in the processes or programs in which they are involved.

The cost to organizations can be both internal and external disengagement, rejection by regulatory bodies and governments, rejection by impacted communities, and damage to the environment. Add to that a wide range of negative human impacts including everything from depression, conflict, suicide, marital breakdown and career paralysis to the loss of intelligence and vision of the brightest people in your business, simply because they mentally and spiritually check out when they come to work.

All this means lost productivity, lost opportunities to grow and prosper, and distracted leaders and workers who no longer feel able to do good work. Leaders and organizations however can gain a strategic advantage by avoiding all this energy and revenue-zapping negativity simply by working together to build a culture of collaboration.

The soul killing command and control also damages families. What if you mattered? What if we mattered? …and it was more valuable to explore together than be seen to be right.

Collaboration is not an event—it's a culture. It's the way we work together. I am a lifelong student of how to get the right people in the right place with the right information in the right mindset to figure out how to conquer challenges and solve conflicts together.

Collaboration is a new field of study and success. Collaboration must evolve. Let's learn together and make our world, communities, and families better.

Google collaboration in 2012 and you will get 278 million results. Google collaboration today and you will get over 550 million results. We are seeking wisdom, skills, and systems for collaboration. With this book and series, I want to build that together.

This is a quote from an OpEd article by Thomas L. Freidman in the *New York Times* from September 27, 2017:

> "When work was predictable, and the change rate was relatively constant, preparation for work merely required the codification and transfer of existing knowledge and predetermined skills to create a stable and deployable work force," explains education consultant Heather McGowan. "Now that the velocity of change has accelerated, due to a combination of exponential growth in technology and globalization, learning can no longer be a set dose of education consumed in the first third of one's life." In this age of accelerations, "the new killer skill set is an agile mind-set that values learning over knowing."

Today's increasing speed of change and increasing complexity make collaboration more important than ever before. No one person can know it all, solve it all, or be it all. Together we are better. Together we go far.

This collaboration guide book is meant to fill the gap between knowing and doing.

"Leadership is difficult. Leadership that depends on collaboration is more difficult."

Rod McKay, Chair of the Heart and Stroke Foundation of Canada and Institute of Corporate Directors Canada

Objectives for this Guide

We are living in a time when our organizations are faced with increasing complexity, speed of change, challenges, differences in demographics, demands for our attention, and distractions. As leaders, we have big dreams and limited resources.

At every level of organizations, leaders are clearly looking for innovative ways to optimize skills, teams, and ways of working together better. As stakeholders and leaders in all organizations around the world, we must make the most effective use of our human resources, time and, money.

Objectives:

1. To inspire readers and participants to more successfully engage teams and capture opportunities

2. To create and maintain an easy-to-use book for leaders and organizations to guide their identification, assessment, selection, leadership, measurement, and completion of projects and initiatives.

3. To understand the 10 Essential Steps to Collaboration, assessments, and leadership tools, and to incorporate them into participant's/reader's projects and professional and personal lives.

4. To learn how to design their projects, teams, resources, and assessments to create an evolving culture that attracts people, resources, and communities.

5. To become more aware of how we, our group, and the world collaborate and may produce better outcomes.

This book is intended as a well-designed collaboration with and for you.

If You Want to Go Fast, Go Alone. If You Want to Go Far, Go Together.

— African proverb

Introduction

Like many of my readers and clients, I work hard to create great results. I coach, consult, speak, write, and lead on collaboration. I actively volunteer for several worthwhile causes including Rotary International, The Heart and Stroke Foundation, and Trails BC. Every organization struggles to achieve more with fewer resources. In response, many leading organizations are collaborating with stakeholders and other organizations so that each can perform what they do best and outsource what they don't.

At the 2017 and 2018 chapter meetings of the Institute of Corporate Directors in Calgary, many not-for-profit organizations realized they are not necessarily competing with one another, and they can collaborate on activities such as outreach, accounting, and leadership/organizational development.

During May 2018, the issues that engaged me professionally included:

- How to successfully advance economic development while protecting the environment and advancing the interests of the community
- How to evolve the energy transition conversation locally and globally
- How to identify, select, teach, and develop next generation leaders and board members
- How to save a project that has suffered from constantly-changing requirements, costs, and designs.
- How to create a regional non-motorized trails alliance
- How to decide on which initiative to champion when there are several attractive ones

These are issues that I hope this guide will work through more productively. I will return to them later in this book.

"With my 38 years of professional work in a not-for-profit and my continued journey with Rotary, great things are always accomplished in a more significant way when there is a focus of collaboration. Of course projects can be completed with a single entity, however the power of collaboration is where real work is accomplished." *Bev Reed, Rotary District 5080 Govenor*

As I was focusing on writing this guide, I was confirmed as a speaker at the June 2018 Rotary International Convention in Toronto. In the past, I have hosted sessions titled "How to Produce Better Outcomes With Well-Designed Collaboration" for several Rotary Club and Rotary District Leadership events.

I originally planned to collaborate with Rotary International on this book, but decided not to for two reasons: 1) Rotary is very firm on their branding and would not allow any use of their logo or any indication this they had any part of this book, and 2) I want to ensure all service organizations, not-for-profits, NGOs, B Corps, and corporations have access and can align with this offering.

Note that the world is evolving our systems, technology, and communications rapidly. We are increasingly employing open technology and crowdsourcing. A powerful example of open/shared technology is Tesla's 2014 announcement that they would not defend their patents.[1] This move works well for organizations that chose to collaborate rather than defend. Innovators like Tesla understand that by sharing their battery and other new technology with their competitors, they will all evolve much faster. Organizations like Rotary that defend and place themselves above their global members create barriers to collaborative innovation.

In early 2018, I conducted a survey of Rotary leaders on their experience of collaboration and their hopes to produce better outcomes. Forty leaders from France (Languedoc), the United States (Washington and Idaho), and Canada (Alberta, British Columbia, and Ontario) provided me with their responses to ten questions. You will find some of the key findings in the appendix. Notably:

1. Only 28% of respondents felt they had access to a concise guide to help them collaborate on their initiatives, and

2. When asked for their top three characteristics of well designed collaborative projects:

Clear Objectives	60%
Clear Communication	56%
Clear Stakeholder Relationships and Accountabilities	36%
Clear Communication Strategy	36%
Clear Focus	32%
Clear End	28%
Clear Leadership	24%
Clear Assessment Process	16%
Clear Accounting	16%

Whether you are a corporate or not-for-profit leader, keep these in your mind as you design your new initiatives. Clear objectives and clear communications are critical.

In this age of anti-social media, distraction, and polarization, positive relationships are critical to your success. And positive relationships require trustworthiness. As highlighted in the appendix section "Advice from My Network," "*A single conversation stifled by a lack of trust doesn't seem that significant, but multiply such a conversation thousands or millions of times, and the macro effects can be profound,*" says innovation guru Victor Hwang.[2]

In this guide, I offer you the basics of my proven processes, templates, and assessments. I encourage you to add to your expertise by reading other books in my *Break Through to Yes* series. This guide is meant to provide a workbook that you can use each time you consider a new initiative or wish to review one already underway or completed.

To help you in very direct ways, this Collaboration Guide delivers:

✓ a clear definition

✓ a checklist

✓ the 10 Essential Steps to Collaboration

✓ the Collaborative Leadership Assessment

✓ a review of your values

✓ a Collaborative Process

✓ a template

✓ a graphic to remind you of self awareness and the 10 Steps

✓ additional resources

✓ advice from my network, and much more

These resources are designed to take you through the entire process.

When people think about collaboration, most don't really know what it is. They think it's getting together. We're going to get together and do something. Not quite sure what that is, what it looks like, who's there, why. Getting together isn't until Step Six of my 10 Essential Steps. Think about that, be a conscious leader, a conscious in-the-moment collaborator—really be aware. Without careful and purposeful design, you are not collaborating—you are only adding more meetings to your busy life.

The 10 Essential Steps to Collaboration are detailed further in the appendix. I believe that many possibilities are left unseen, untapped, and unclaimed. Together we are better. Together we can do a far better job. So let's get out there and collaborate more effectively to produce better outcomes.

Values and Ethics

"Without an ethical system in place, all actions are equally acceptable, and no one is safe from his neighbor."[3]

When we start to work together in diverse demographic groups, a critical early step is to explore values and ethics. By reaching agreement on how we behave together and what our values are, we reduce the potential for future conflict and misdirection.

Considering any current or future collaboration, what are the values that we agree will guide us? Ensure that you, your organization, and your collaborative actively discuss and agree on your values. This will help you make choices going forward. Ethics are the application of your values. Do you act ethically? Does your team? Do people and organizations that you align with?

Here are some values and interests that may be useful:

- Respect
- Trust
- Environmental protection
- Creation of positive cumulative effects
- Reduction of cumulative adverse effects
- Healthy lifestyles for our communities
- Transparency
- Accountability
- Openness
- Curiosity
- Innovation

- Education
- Diversity
- Low costs
- Accessible to all
- Fairness
- Focus on the future
- Creativity
- Inclusion
- Community building
  [Add you own]
-
-
-
-

Never answer a question framed from your opponent's point of view. Always reframe the question to fit your values and your frames. This may make you uncomfortable, since normal discourse styles require you to directly answer questions posed. That is a trap.

Practice changing frames…
Remember there are a lot of guidelines.
But there are only four really important ones:

Show respect
Respond by reframing
Think and talk at the level of values
Say what you believe.[4]

At the Energy Disruptors Unite Conference in Calgary, Canada in May 2018, experts on energy transitions, blockchain, augmented intelligence, autonous vehicles, machine thinking, and business innovation included Sir Richard Branson, Roz Savage, Steve Williams, and many more. During most every session over the two days, one thing that many of the experts and successful innovators agreed upon is that without clearly-stated and shared values, all can run amok quickly and opportunities will be lost. Innovation and collaboration, without a foundation of agreed upon organizational values, can be a dangerous thing.

A Graphic Overview

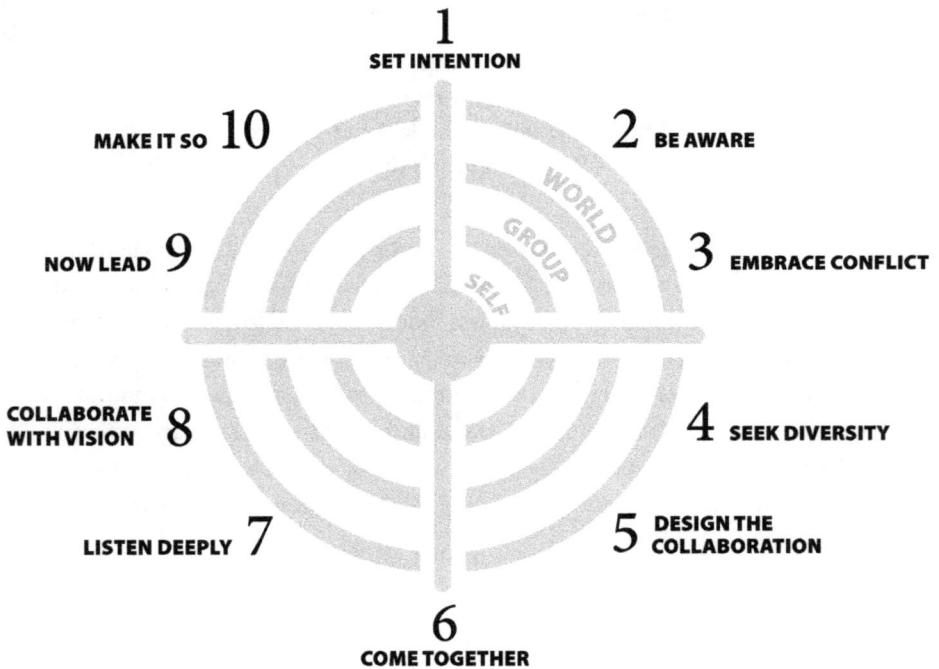

1
SET INTENTION

MAKE IT SO 10

2 BE AWARE

NOW LEAD 9

3 EMBRACE CONFLICT

WORLD
GROUP
SELF

COLLABORATE WITH VISION 8

4 SEEK DIVERSITY

LISTEN DEEPLY 7

5 DESIGN THE COLLABORATION

6
COME TOGETHER

Mindfully review this graphic representation of the key ideas in this guide. It focuses you on:

- Hitting your target
- Developing your self awareness as a collaborative leader
- Appreciating how you show up in your group and in your world
- Using the 10 Essential Steps to Collaboration, and
- Knowing how to produce better outcomes

This graphic will be used through this guide to bring you to focus.

What is Collaboration?

Merriam Webster defines collaborate as: "to work with another person or group in order to achieve or do something." This could refer to a meeting or what a football team does. I prefer this definition:

"Collaboration is highly diversified teams working together inside and outside a company with the purpose to create value by improving innovation, customer relationships, and efficiency while leveraging technology for effective interactions in the virtual and physical space." Cisco Blog, *The Platform, Collaboration: What Does It Really Mean?* by Carlos Dominguez, February 9, 2011 *(Dominguez, 2011)*

Let's make a joint proclamation that we value collaboration as a powerful way of leading. Collaboration isn't an act—it is the way we lead. To collaborate isn't simply to work together, it is an organizational culture.

We see the potential of true collaboration in my friend Kenneth Cloke's book *The Dance of Opposites; Explorations in Mediation, Dialogue and Conflict Resolution Systems Design.*

"Fundamentally, the role of leaders in an organizational democracy is to expand the number of degrees of organizational freedom and orchestrate these elements to create learning relationships that link people across artificial boundaries. Organizational separations and divisions that are not integrated produce role confusions, feelings of irresponsibility, misunderstandings, stereotypes, conflicts, and internal dissension, which can be used to justify and rationalize bureaucratic divisions and hierarchical control. Every organizational division is simply a different way of understanding, processing and solving common problems. The task of democratic leaders is to reveal the whole to each of its parts and to integrate the concerns of all into a single synergistic, strategically integrated whole.

Collaboration, democracy, and self-management are prerequisites for evolution to higher levels of organizational development based on synergy, community, and strategic integration. Through these processes, it becomes possible to build creative, motivated, high performance, self-managing teams that harmonize and orchestrate a wide range of organizational skills, strategies, systems, processes, and relationships to produce synergistic results.

Creating a fully democratic, collaborative, self-managing organization requires more than fragmented, step-by-step, tactical reforms. It requires integrated, holistic, strategic transformations that increase diversity, complexity, synergy, and interconnectedness and challenge everyone to operate at their highest levels of effectiveness. In the process, employees need to become owners of the organizations they are changing and of the process by which they are changed."

With my 10 Essential Steps to Collaboration, developed later in this guide, I provide a step-by-step approach to creating well designed and successful projects and initiatives.

Why Collaboration Fails

When you look at the cover of my book, what do the shaded letters spell?

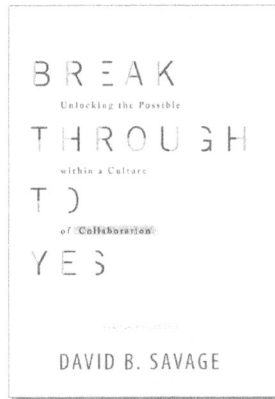

B R E A K
Unlocking the Possible

T H R O U G H
within a Culture

T O
of Collaboration

Y E S

DAVID B. SAVAGE

EGOS are the greatest barrier to effective collaboration.

Here are other barriers, as stated by Ken Cloke:

- Neglecting to involve those who are most immediately impacted by the problem
- Not making collaborative improvements in the design of systems, processes, relationships, communications, and technology
- Not reducing or eliminating bureaucratic work that takes time and energy from collaboration efforts
- Inability to visualize what collaboration is intended to achieve, or using it to pursue unclear priorities or vague objectives
- Lack of clarity about how to put it into practice
- Failing to transform existing cultures, processes, and relationships, and significantly alter day-to-day behaviors[5]

A Culture of Collaboration

I invite you to think of collaboration as a culture. Too often, collaboration fails when a leader misuses their power and names collaboration when their actions belie manipulation. Collaboration as "the way we do things around here" is the most effective approach. And there is no end to a collaborative culture. That system is always in continuous improvement, measurement, feedback, engagement, conflict, evolution… In my book, *Break Through To Yes: Unlocking the Possible within a Culture of Collaboration,* I explore and promote my strong belief that a real, insightful, and successful culture of collaboration creates breakthrough thinking, systems, and products.

The Rainforest: The Secret to Building the Next Silicon Valley[6] is a tremendous gift to leaders wishing to design and build an organizational culture that truly innovates and succeeds.

> "… a radical new theory to explain the phenomenon of innovation eco-systems—social networks that generate extraordinary creativity and output. The authors challenge basic assumptions that economists have held for over a century. *The Rainforest* will transform the way you think about technology, business, and leadership."

One of the key ideas in *the Rainforest* is that innovation and great success doesn't come from being smarter, wealthier, or any of the expected factors. Great innovation and success comes from those that collaborate best. An organizational ecosystem that features mutual support, high levels of trust and engagement, and more than anything, connects resources freely (not competitively). Rainforest groups are growing across the world.[7]

You and your organization are invited to publicly commit to and sign the Rainforest Social Contract:

1. I am joining a global community of people who share a common faith in the culture of innovation and entrepreneurship. I am open to meeting anyone in this community.

2. I understand that I will receive valuable help from others for free or at a very low cost.

3. I agree to "pay forward" whatever positive benefits I receive. For every introduction I get, I will provide an introduction to another person. For every hour of advice I receive, I will give an hour of advice to someone else. For every risk someone takes with me, I will take a risk with a different person.

4. I will give trust to others before expecting to receive trust in return. I will treat everyone fairly. I will take advantage of no one.

5. I will bring people together, as none of us is as smart as all of us.

6. I will dream, experiment, iterate, and persist. I understand that mistakes and failure are acceptable ways of testing new ideas.

7. I will open myself to learning from others. I will help nurture learning in others.

8. Each person is a role model for everyone else. I will live these ideals as a member of the Rainforest community."

As leaders, parents, grandparents and community members, we are concerned about the social interaction of the future generations of leaders. Too often, we see isolation, judgments, aggressive behavior, and ignorance on social media. And we worry about augmented intelligence by "learning" computers.

In March 2016, Microsoft wanted to experiment with a social bot named Tay. Tay was designed to communicate and learn from Twitter interactions with young adult women. "It took less than 24 hours. Microsoft had released its latest experiment with artificial intelligence: a Twitter bot named Tay that was designed to research and foster "conversational understanding." But Tay learned too much, much too young."[8] Within twenty-four hours on Twitter, Tay became rude, aggressive, judgmental and racist.

As leaders, we are responsible to influence, mentor, coach, manage, engage and serve as role models to the future generations. How might you save a young leader from being "Tay-zered"?

Are you actively evolving your organization's culture of collaboration? How will you measure, redesign, incentify and celebrate your people as they make it so? Will you sign the Rainforest Social Contract? What will you do today to serve as a role model for others?

A Collaborative Process

You must slow down before you can go fast.
You must be courageous.
Those leaders that run ahead, often die alone.
Working in silos simply destroys possibility.

"In the collaborative leadership model, a collaborative leader facilitates dialog ensuring all voices are heard and counted. A collaborative leader considers the past, the present, and the future, allowing space for dialog to consider where we've been, where we are now, and where we wish to go. A collaborative leader clarifies assumptions knowing that it is misunderstandings that derail the process. Collaborative leaders must be both humble and courageous. Humble because they know that they alone do not have all the answers. Courageous because they must trust that it takes the knowledge of many to create meaningful and sustainable results. They work toward consensus knowing that any solution will fail unless there is agreement between all. For collaboration to work, people must be accountable and responsible to the collaborative process. Doing what they say and saying what they do while acting with integrity. This process takes time, but the results are amazing and well worth the investment!" *Denise Chartrand* [9]

Key Elements

There are key elements to design your initiatives.

What is your Why?

> "There are only two ways to influence human behavior: you can manipulate it or you can inspire it. Very few people or companies can clearly articulate WHY they do WHAT they do. By WHY, I mean your purpose, cause, or belief—WHY does your company exist? WHY do you get out of bed every morning? And WHY should anyone care? People don't buy WHAT you do, they buy WHY you do it." *Simon Sinek*[10]

Because a project has been proposed, because a passionate strong member of your organization champions it, because you have done this project for several years, because …. Are not inspiring "Whys".

> "Remember this, we only really pursue goals that are personally important to us. So, your key priorities will in large measure define your WHY. If you can have business, project, and personal priorities connected, then success is at hand. When your project priorities reflect your personal priorities, then your work becomes a purpose, you will be 'on fire', you'll be 'crushing it!' If they don't—that's when it feels like a job and you are just trading hours for dollars." *Barry Wilson*[11]

Review your own organization's objectives, strategic plan, membership, community needs and the resources you can bring as you consider your Why. More powerfully, does this project inspire, attract, and serve in ways superior to other projects?

> **"Gettin' good players is easy.**
> **Gettin' 'em to play together is the hard part."**
> *Casey Stengel*

What are the deliverables, accountabilities, and measurements that you will use to track the initiative? Is it feasible? Do you have the systems in place to manage the project effectively (money, people, outreach, liability, …)?

Project management is a complete field of business. Over the past millennium, leaders have developed great systems, budgets, communications, and analytics to ensure projects are completed as planned, as budgeted and on time. Yet according to Howard W. Ashcraft Jr., most construction projects in North

America, small ones and billion dollar ones, have significant cost overruns. That is why Ashcraft is a leader in Integrative Project Delivery.[12]

In a February 2018 presentation on Integrated/Collaborative Project Delivery at the Calgary Petroleum Club, Ashcraft asserted:

A Few Truths on Project Management

- Hierarchical management is not effective in complex dynamic environments
- Individual optimization leads to conflict, delay, and inefficiency

While Collaborative Integrated Project Delivery leads to:

- Early involvement of key participants
- Jointly shared risk/rewards based on the project outcome
- Joint project management
- Limited liability amongst the team members
- Cost guarantees
- Dynamic problem solving

Think about teams that are agile, effective, trust one another, have shared risks and rewards, and are continually evolving.

When things are changing quickly, do we have the tools and commitment to communicate and resolve issues in the moment? Or must we write it all down and wait for the next meeting that already is too-far distant and has a too-full an agenda? Do your project teams compare what is happening with what was planned, and have full permission to communicate, engage, and make changes as they are needed?

While most organization's projects can be limited in time and resources, some projects often take decades and cost in the hundreds of millions of dollars. So let's not treat project management lightly. Let's not use tools that are widely used but are often ineffective. Going forward, we must lead using the best practices available to us.

> **"Coming together is the beginning. Keeping together is progress. Working together is success."**
>
> *Henry Ford*[13]

Key Success Factors that each project must be clear on:

1. What is our WHY?
2. How does this initiative serve our WHY?
3. What is the system we agree to operate within?
4. Who decides?
5. How do you decide?
6. Who pays?
7. Who leads? And for what parts?
8. Who owns it?
9. What are the accountabilities for everyone?
10. Who has permission to act immediately and to what extent?
11. How do you resolve conflict?
12. Who benefits?
13. What did we learn?
14. How do you evolve your decision making and leadership for future initiatives based on this experience?
15. How will we celebrate success together?

How You Show up

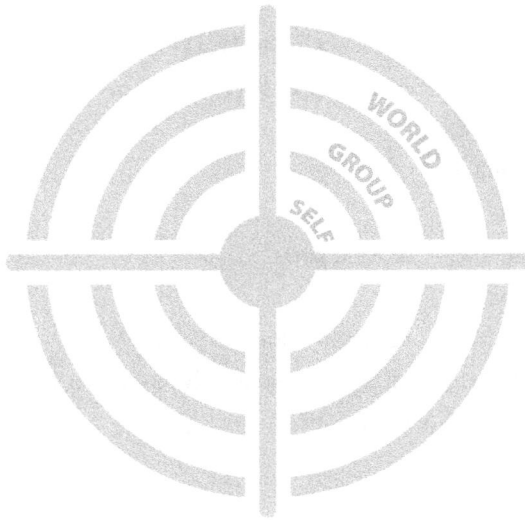

"I know it is possible for leaders to use their power and
influence, their insight and compassion, to lead people back
to an understanding of who we are as human beings, to create
the conditions for our basic human qualities of generosity,
contribution, community, and love to be evoked no matter what.
I know it is possible to experience grace and joy in the midst of
tragedy and loss. I know it is possible to create Islands of Sanity in
the midst of wildly disruptive seas. I know it is possible because
I have worked with leaders over many years in places that knew
chaos and breakdown long before this moment. And I have studied
enough history to know that such leaders always arise when they
are most needed. Now it's our turn." [14]

Here is my challenge to you:

- How do you show up in the three levels of leadership: self, group, and world?
- Do you show up differently in the three levels?
- Reflect on the ways and behaviors in your leadership that you integrate the whole.
- Reflect on the ways and behaviors of business leaders that do not integrate the whole.
- Reflect on your beliefs on what the outcomes of both approaches most often create.
- What are you mindful of, based on these reflections?
- How might you change the outcomes of your business decisions and initiatives by utilizing a more holistic approach to collaboration?
- Notice that there is a clear connection between self, group, and world. Who you are in all three must be in integrity.

> **"Collaboration is a beautiful opportunity to combine one's strengths with another's different strengths creating mutual successes."**
>
> *Don Pegneaud, Begno, Paradox of Life*

"Through interviews, teaching, and consulting, they uncovered what distinguishes the most effective leaders. Simply put, the answer lies in how leaders lead themselves and take accountability for their personal and professional growth in today's challenging environment. At the heart of Centered Leadership lies the practice of self-awareness and choice. The ability of leaders to be mindful and at choice in the moment helps them tap into purpose and vision (Meaning), shift habitual patterns into a learning stance (Framing), create collective relationships (Connecting), step up with intention (Engaging), and sustain transformational growth (Energizing)."[15]

A leader is most successful when she or he focuses on the whole, not on their power, not on their compensation, not on their legacy. They're more successful when they do it together. It's the only way. A woman I have a great regard for is Margaret Wheatley. "When leaders take back power, when they act as heroes and saviors, they end up exhausted, overwhelmed, and deeply stressed. We can't allow them to be overwhelmed, we need to support them and they need to support us."[16]

So what do we see? It takes time to change the culture from command and control where power is isolated and shift it to collaboration. I'm a visual person and I enjoy road biking. Road biking is something I took up about several years ago. I do it poorly—slowly, but I do it. I'm out there on the road. I've ridden in five Gran Fondos and have had a lot of fun.

Think of collaboration as the peloton in the Tour de France. In a peloton, what I realized is, the group pulls me along. Literally, if I can tuck in to the back of that group (often when they're passing me) they're slipstreaming… we're slipstreaming, we're all faster together. Literally, you could feel it in that peloton on the side of a road. It is fantastic. And in the peloton, notice that a person doesn't stay at the front of the peloton for more than a few minutes, maybe ten minutes, because otherwise they would be overwhelmed. The stress and exhaustion come if you're trying to break the wind for everybody else. So you rotate.

Think of yourself in your organization, your family, your nation as a peloton. Don't give away your power. Don't ignore your own wisdom. Don't be afraid. Step in. Vision what you choose and create it together. Contact me at **davidbsavage.com**, I'd love to hear how this is working for you… what your thoughts are. What is the project or skill that you want to develop further? How might I help you connect to that network… connect you, challenge you, include you? Look for ways to share power.[17]

The 10 Essential Steps to Collaboration

> "…organizations hit walls of resistance (partly of their own creation) which prevent collaborations succeeding. The problem is not with the idea of collaboration, but the way many have attempted to apply it. The solution lies in preparing your own organization for the change."
>
> *Jonathan Webb*[18]

In my 42-year career in leadership, negotiation, dispute resolution, joint ventures, and business development, I have found that leaders and members rarely understand what true collaboration is. Every day, we hear "collaboration," "we are collaborating," "we are collaborative" … and rarely is that true. Collaboration does not mean meeting. Collaboration, too often, is manipulation. Collaboration is not an opportunity to get others sold on your ideas.

My friend, Rod McKay, respected Canadian business person, Chapter Chair of the Institute of Corporate Directors (Calgary), and Chair of the Heart and Stroke Foundation of Canada told me:

"Leadership is difficult. Leadership that depends on collaboration is more difficult… Collaboration is one of the most misused words today. It is thrown out in conversations without regard to what it actually means."

Collaboration deigned and performed well is an opportunity to explore interests, involve diverse perspectives, create dreams, innovate, generate collective wisdom, and capture possibilities that no one alone could.

A significant focus of my career and this book is to help people collaborate to create better outcomes than any person in a silo or alone could realize.

Collaboration is an exciting and evolving field of leadership.

That is why I created the 10 Essential Steps to Collaboration as a clear and concise guide to help us better design our projects and significantly enhance the probability of real success.

10 MAKE IT SO
POSITIVELY CHANGE THE ENERGY AND THE FUTURE TOGETHER

1 SET INTENTION
DECLARE YOUR HONEST PURPOSE

2 BE AWARE
ENGAGE OTHERS WITH AN OPEN HEART

9 NOW LEAD
WITH PURPOSE AND ACCOUNTABILITY

3 EMBRACE CONFLICT
SEEK OUT THOSE THAT SPEAK OUT

THE 10 STEPS

BUILD YOUR CULTURE, LEARN TOGETHER, & CREATE BREAKTHROUGH THINKING

8 COLLABORATE WITH VISION
TAP INTO THE COLLECTIVE WISDOM.

4 SEEK DIVERSITY
BRING IN MANY PERSPECTIVES

7 LISTEN DEEPLY
REALIZE WHAT WANTS TO BE HEARD BUT IS NOT SPOKEN

6 COME TOGETHER
ENGAGE WITH RESPECT AND TRUST

5 DESIGN THE COLLABORATION
IMAGINE SUCCESS AND CREATE THE RIGHT CONTAINER

From *Break Through to Yes: Unlocking the Possible within a Culture of Collaboration*[19]

1. Set Intention

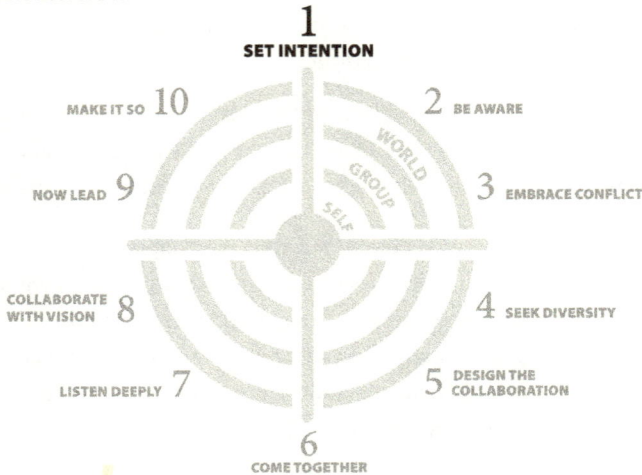

1
SET INTENTION

MAKE IT SO 10

2 BE AWARE

NOW LEAD 9

3 EMBRACE CONFLICT

COLLABORATE WITH VISION 8

4 SEEK DIVERSITY

LISTEN DEEPLY 7

5 DESIGN THE COLLABORATION

6
COME TOGETHER

WORLD
GROUP
SELF

What is your true intention of this project?

Far too often, we rush into things without stopping to ask: what is my purpose? What is my intention? Even worse, often we think we know the answer before we start. Can you state your intention to your team in one sentence that includes your Why and your Vision?

In Step 8, Collaborate with Vision, you will generate a greater and more inclusive vision. Here in Step 1, what is your own vision that will invite others to collaborate with you? Write down, with artwork or by creating a collage, paint your picture of success.

"Personal purpose, in essence, is a lifetime journey. Many individuals make the mistake of believing once they "find themselves," there is no need to further develop or strengthen their personal purpose. This is where a lot of trouble begins for people—where disengagement or disaffection can creep in. We ought to yearn for new experiences, knowledge and acumen whether through projects, roles, rotations, mentors, further education, and so on. People should consciously choose whether to operate with truth or dishonesty, with openness or intolerance, with grit or timidity, with love or hostility. Every decision—every day of our being—is a decision on how we choose to act with personal purpose...or not."[20]

2. Be Aware

1 SET INTENTION
10 MAKE IT SO
2 BE AWARE
9 NOW LEAD
3 EMBRACE CONFLICT
8 COLLABORATE WITH VISION
4 SEEK DIVERSITY
7 LISTEN DEEPLY
5 DESIGN THE COLLABORATION
6 COME TOGETHER

WORLD
GROUP
SELF

What are the outside influences and inside interests that may encourage or discourage your project (i.e. make it successful or fail)?

Before you begin, be aware of the values, interests, personalities, and perspectives that you will want to include. Also, be aware of the people that will fight to defeat you. Just because a group of people appear to be working for the good of the community doesn't mean everyone in the community will support and engage in the collaboration. Self-interest most often trumps public interest.

Who are the people and interests that may defeat your intention?

Be Aware is not only about others, it is about you. How aware are your leadership and impact on your own life, your organization and our world?

3. Embrace Conflict

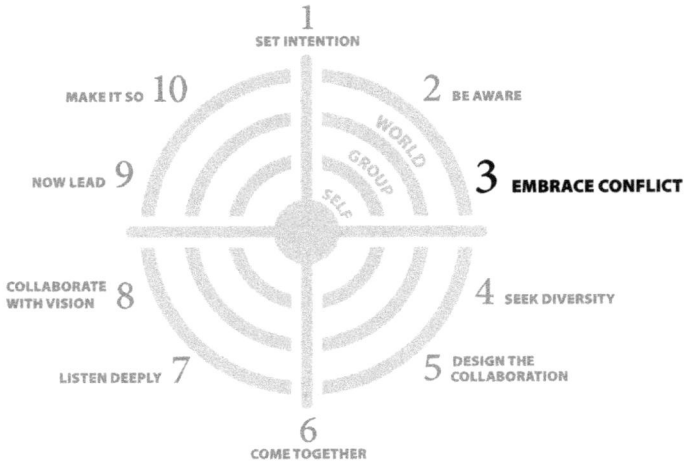

Do we have people involved that will speak up when we disagree?

What are our rules of engagement?

What are our agreements on how we resolve conflict?

Those who disagree have much to teach us. The value of conflict is to gain understanding, trust, and build relationship. I embrace conflict because underneath there are real interests and real values that must be understood and not bypassed. I would far rather work with people in conflict than people who are unengaged and passive aggressive.

Who are those in conflict with us and how do we get them involved?

Do you need some different strategies to improve your business partnerships? Are you looking for ideas to deal productively with conflict and get on with business? With my Company to Company Dispute Resolution resources, you can better embrace, learn from, and succeed through conflict.[21]

4. Seek Diversity

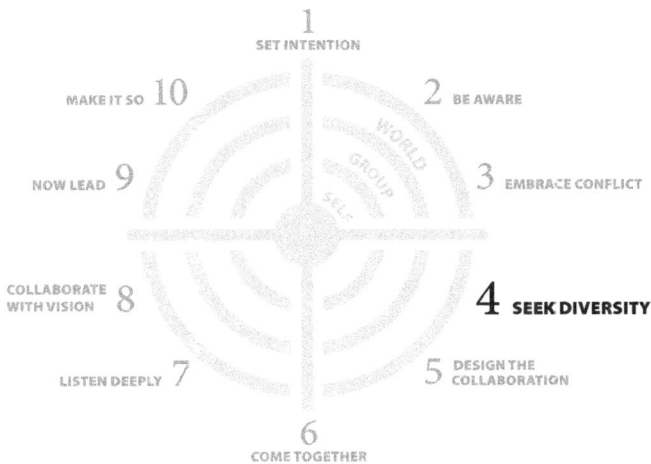

Make certain that those you gather do not all look like you and believe what you believe.

When an organization thinks about collaborating, it often assembles the usual suspects and their managers, who have demonstrated a willing- ness to get along and arrive at consensus.

But where are the people who see things differently? If the group norms dictate that you must be nice and that you must support some project, then save your energy. The "collaboration" will be shallow and too comfortable.

Given a specific challenge, project, or conflict, you must consciously decide what expertise, personalities, backgrounds, and strengths are required. Those who have different perspectives, expertise, demographics, and personalities are valuable.

How are you seeking out those differences?

"Diversity is critical for organization's ability to innovate and adapt in a fast-changing environment. Some of the most successful entrepreneurs and most admired leaders will tell you the same thing. Diversity is essential to growth and prosperity of any company: diversity of perspectives, experiences, cultures, genders, and age. Why? Because diversity breeds innovation. And innovation breeds business success."[22]

5. Design the Collaboration

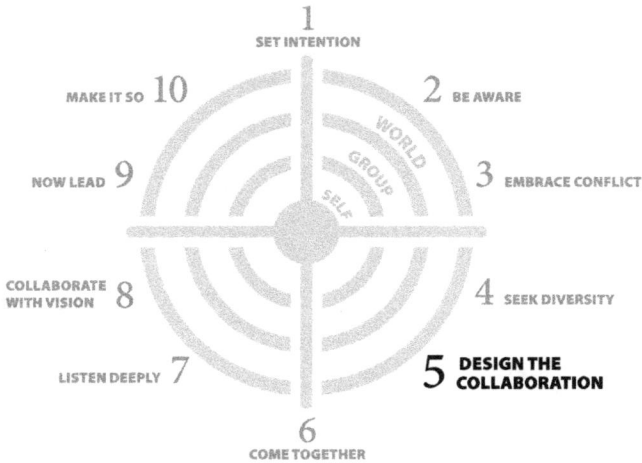

Carefully and mindfully create the right container so the right people have the right resources and the right space with a clear objective to get to the best outcome.

Is the space a forest, a circle, an online virtual meeting? Or are you a "sage on the stage" with willing devotees?

Notice in the 10 Step process, we have arrived at Step Five and we have yet to get to the place that most leaders start their collaborative efforts. Intention, awareness, embracing conflict, ensuring diversity, and designing the collaboration are necessary steps to success. When we rush into it and skip over these conscious preparatory actions, we greatly reduce the probability of breakthrough results. Building an agreement, a business relationship, and a culture of collaborative management is significant and deserves far more preparation, planning, and engagement than we most often give it.

6. Come Together

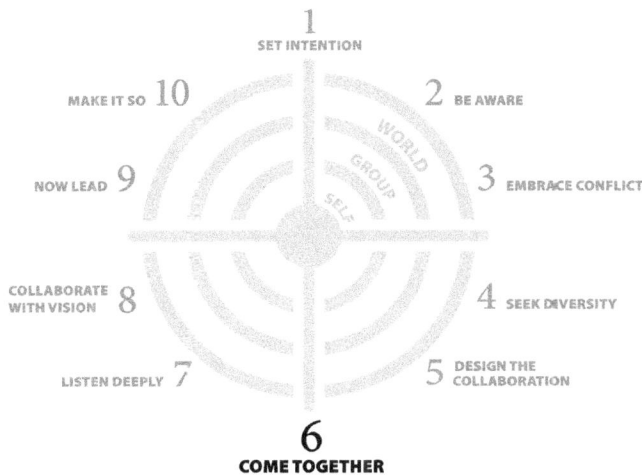

Deep listening and active engagement are critical. Everyone has a voice. Everyone must have ears.

When you come together, changing the mindset, body set, and heart set is important. This cannot be another "bloody meeting." Transition from what you had been doing into a fresh, open and creative energetic space. For most, simply reminding everyone of the intention, purpose, and vision may be enough. Some may go outside into nature. Some may use a room that contains artwork, music, and large windows—not the usual meeting space.

Ritual is important but has been much ignored over the past 50 years. Ritual beginnings and endings to collaborative groups serve as important markers to our brain, heart, spirit, and body that something different is happening that we need to be open to and aware of.

Realize that collaboration, coaching, dispute resolution, and most transformative processes are step changes. They will fail if they are seen as "one time" events. Building, holding, and challenging ourselves into a culture of collaboration is very powerful and necessary.

7. Listen Deeply

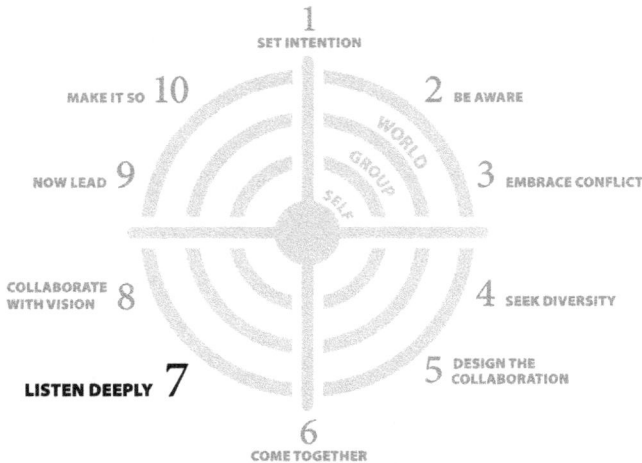

Focus on what is being communicated. Leave the distractions alone.

There is a reason we have two ears, two eyes, but only one mouth.

Early in my career, when I was participating in boardroom discussions, I would spend most of my time thinking how best to state what I wanted the others to understand. This took me out of the discussion into my own head, and away from the discussion at hand. In doing so, I missed so much opportunity to hear the others and build on the conversations. With my experience and confidence, I soon learned that by listening first and talking later, my contributions were far more valued. By having faith that I knew what I wished others to understand after hearing them, I could craft my communications appropriately.

"Seek first to understand. Then to be understood." Stephen Covey, *The 7 Habits of Highly Effective People*.[23]

As a professional coach, I have been trained to:

- Listen at level one: listen to my internal voice.
- Listen at level two: listen with intense focus on the client.
- Listen at level three: sense the entire room and its energy.

Try all three levels of listening.

8. Collaborate with Vision

If you only focus on the problem, you will never see the solution.

If a player focuses on the net behind the goalie, their probability of scoring is significantly improved.

Be bold in your vision. Look at where you wish to be. Dream about how that feels, what the air is like, and what you see there. Dream big. Then work back from there to see the steps that need to be taken to make it happen. When I am coaching executives, often I must shift them from the day-to-day tension, challenge, and frustration. When we explore their values and their vision of themselves and their company in five years' time, they look beyond the collisions in front of them. They become more strongly motivated. Setting the strategic plan is far easier looking back from success than looking forward past obstacles.

What is your finish line? What do you feel being there? Who is with you? What are you doing? What is your gift? What do you need to do to start building that future?

9. Now Lead

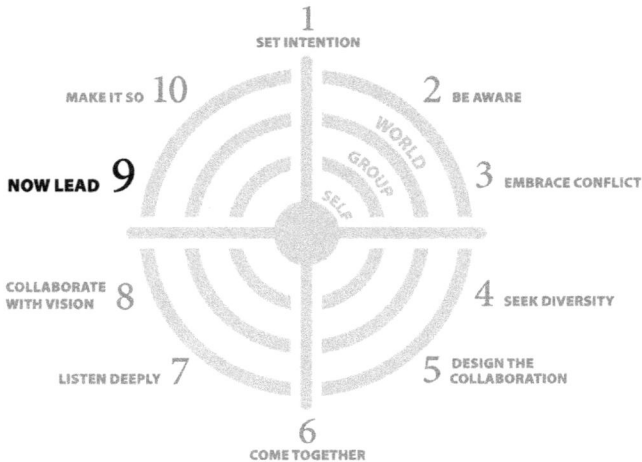

This is the time to step into true leadership.

Once you have been through the first eight Steps, this is the time you get moving by taking charge.

Leadership by consensus is deadly.

Effective collaboration requires the strong leadership brought about by such dimensions as clarity of vision, decision-making capabilities, emotional intelligence, and engendering of trust. A strong leader demands accountability from his whole team, regardless of who is on the team.

Accountability fulfils purpose. What is your and your organization's purpose? What is the essential "why?" you are answering? If you and your organization failed, what would be lost to the outside world? We have talked about how and why collaboration fails or succeeds. But how might you learn from that experience to enhance your probability of success in your present work and in the future?

For a collaboration to achieve and even exceed its goals, everyone, in his own way, must lead. No one can sit idly as a bystander. Everyone, by utilizing their skills and networks, and so executing on their part of the plan, has a contribution to make.

> "A good leader needs to be a good listener.
> You're not gaining much if you listen only to yourself."
>
> *Richard Branson*

10. Make It So

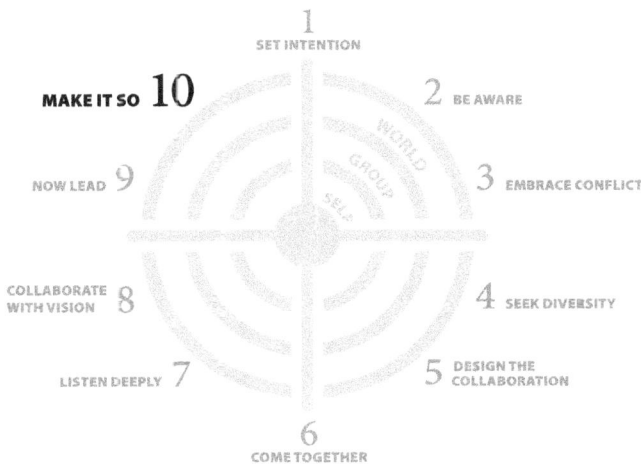

The circle completes when the plan is well designed, people have clear responsibilities and authority, and everyone is accountable.

There is a fine balance required to be a successful collaborative leader. At once you are called to be open and inclusive while at the same time taking charge. People need to believe in their leader and in their team. Is the best leader the rock star or the leader who places others in the recognition spotlight? I say both. Each is optimal in certain circumstances.

To "Make It So," you will need to design and follow through on:

- ✓ Accountabilities
- ✓ Effective reporting
- ✓ Continuous improvement, post-mortem, what worked, what didn't, how are we together now, what is needed for future collaborations
- ✓ Building the collaborative muscle of your organization
- ✓ Learning from successes and failures
- ✓ Using accepted evaluation tools, Collaborative Leadership and Team Development 360 Assessment (see **http://www.davidbsavage. com/360-degree-assessments/**)
- ✓ Integration—changing the existing ways we do things to capitalize on the collaborative process, outcomes, and the organization's rules of engagement. Build your culture of collaboration according to circumstance and need.

Richard Schultz of Wisdom Ways views the 10 Essential Steps in these frames:

- ✓ Vision and purpose: Step 1 Set Intention
- ✓ Leadership: Steps 2 to 4, Be Aware, Embrace Conflict and Seek Diversity.
- ✓ Container: Step 5 Design the Collaboration
- ✓ Process with Stakeholders: Step 6 to 8, Come Together, Listen Deeply and Collaborate with Vision
- ✓ Management: Step 9 and 10, Now Lead and Make It So

A Checklist

Key Questions Before You Complete your Design

Consider any of these key questions (from Step 5, Design the Collaboration) to help you establish your own process.

	QUESTION	YOUR DESIGN ANSWERS
1	Why are you really doing this?	
2	Why would others choose to join us?	
3	What is the real question that needs to be answered?	
4	Are the participants' priorities complementary or conflicting?	
5	What are the alternatives and how do you compare and choose?	
6	What are the current and necessary preconditions?	

	QUESTION	YOUR DESIGN ANSWERS
7	Do you trust the others? Is trust an issue for others? What is needed?	
8	Is their time line similar?	
9	What are the underlying interests?	
10	What is the best alternative to collaborating for everyone individually?	
11	What will the rules of engagement be?	
12	How do you encourage disagreement and freedom to speak without invoking negative emotions and responses?	
13	What about confidentiality?	
14	What resources do you need to make this work?	
15	What are the metrics and measurables you seek to create?	
16	What are the styles of the participants and how do you ensure they are included?	

	QUESTION	YOUR DESIGN ANSWERS
17	Who has the authority to agree and how will they be engaged?	
18	How do you support one another in getting the ultimate result approved within the respective organizations?	
19	How will this serve you, the others, and the organization beyond the specific topic?	
20	What are the threats? What will pull people away?	
21	How will people and organizations be accountable?	
22	What is it we wish to capture as we go through the collaboration?	
23	What is the physical space that will encourage creativity?	
24	Will there be times when the group needs to shrink and/or expand?	
25	How will we communicate with those not directly involved?	
26	Where and how can we incorporate art, music, poetry, dance, and humor into our circle to engage all parts of our brains, creativity, and more?	

	QUESTION	YOUR DESIGN ANSWERS
27	What roles do we ask people to play?	
28	Who is the facilitator or meeting lead?	
29	Who will the champions be and when might they change roles within the process?	
30	What do the executive/stakeholders need, from us and others, to be our champions?	
31	Shall we invite open source collaboration from experts and others out-side our own organization, team, culture, or nation?	

On the next page is a blank template for the 10 Essential Steps to Collaboration for you to complete for each initiative/project you wish to design to guide you and your team effectively. Feel free to copy these forms and write in your answers for each initiative.

		WHAT
1	Set Intention	
2	Be Aware	
3	Embrace Conflict	
4	Seek Diversity	
5	Design the Collaboration	
6	Come Together	
7	Listen Deeply	
8	Collaborate with Vision	
9	Now Lead	
10	Make It So	

An Assessment[24]

> "First-time collaborators have not developed a trust in the
> process to create the best decisions. We know the process allows
> the kind of input and caution to create not only sustainable but
> regenerative relationships and GOOD decisions, but until someone
> has seen that happen there is skepticism and concern. I have found
> two kinds of concerns. There is the "BUT I'm the expert..." concern,
> and there is the "Why should I help them...?" concern. Either will
> get in the way of the deliberately gentle, honest, open, and specific
> talk necessary to ensure results and success from collaboration."
>
> *Dr. Nancy Love. Pulse Institute*

How might you assess the state of your organization's collaborative ecosystem? Think of how beneficial an assessment would be that pertains specifically to your organization, the particular challenges and opportunities you face, your connection to your collaborative networks, and where the strengths and weaknesses are that you will address. Consider this an evolutionary assessment that you check back to every three to six months. This will be an organizational success indicator.

This will be a tool that your team, department, organization, and network can assess from a "we" perspective.

I offer you an assessment. I invite you to customize it for your own organization, add/subtract aspects, and continuously develop over time. The order of the aspects/questions/topics may be reorganized, prioritized, or randomized. In this assessment, I consider the elements of essential collaboration and the expertise of your network. Rank your team, specific to one project initially, on a scale of 1 to 5 with 1 representing not effective and 5 representing very effective. I recommend you do this individually then combine the comments and average the totals. The order of the questions is meant to be random.

A much more complete version of my Collaborative Leadership and Team Development Assessment is, also, available online as an application at **http://www.davidbsavage.com/360-degree-assessments/**.[25]

#	ASPECT	RANK	REMARKS/ RECOMMENDATIONS
1	We start with the end in mind and work back to today.		
2	We have positively experienced the value of collaboration together.		
3	We understand our clients' needs.		
4	Our clients/communities actively collaborate with us.		
5	We seek out those that disagree/ speak out with different ideas.		
6	We have a clearly stated set of agreed-upon principles for working together that respects the ethical values of our members.		
7	We are clear on our intention for each collaboration.		
8	We ensure a variety of perspectives are represented.		
9	We identify conflicting interests and address them.		
10	We listen and listen and listen.		

#	ASPECT	RANK	REMARKS/ RECOMMENDATIONS
11	We have clearly established the "Why."		
12	We have the necessary resources to accomplish the objectives.		
13	We have the support of those outside our team.		
14	We have clear accountabilities for the team and each member.		
15	We have a transparent structure and reporting.		
16	We have established team work communication principles.		
17	We respect all members and "have their back."		
18	We trust one another, the team and the network.		
19	When one of us believes something is not right, we listen to them.		
20	We share information to increase understanding, encourage discussion, and enhance participation in decision-making.		

#	ASPECT	RANK	REMARKS/ RECOMMENDATIONS
21	We have appropriate education and support for that training.		
22	We have effective team processes including collaborative decision-making.		
23	We co-create a climate of shared leadership and collaborative practice.		
24	We take time to have fun at work and to maintain our collective health and individual wellbeing.		
25	We work in a variety of places inside and outside our organization and inside and outside offices.		
26	We are aware of and take steps to identify situations that are likely to lead to disagreements or conflicts, including role ambiguity, power gradients, and differences in goals		
27	We know and understand strategies to deal with conflict.		
29	Team members have guidelines for addressing disagreements.		
30	When we hold team meetings, they are purpose driven and focused on the end result.		
31	We spend real time with those that we are serving or working with.		

#	ASPECT	RANK	REMARKS/ RECOMMENDATIONS
32	We ensure that when a member's involvement is not needed they are free to disengage and remain informed.		
33	We are consistently inclusive of all team members, touching base, keeping those who may not be directly involved in "the loop."		
34	We challenge ourselves to bigger dreams.		
35	We meet our time deadlines.		
36	We meet our budgets and forecasts.		
37	We see that different people lead at different times.		
38	We are recognized and compensated with regard to how we collaborate and the success of our outcomes.		
39	We see ourselves as a strong, successful, and true team.		
40	We are highly regarded by our clients/ investors/ community.		
	Total		

With this assessment, each aspect must then be addressed and ways to improve identified. A more useful exercise (beyond what the scores may indicate) is to discuss openly the results with the team and ascertain where improvements and celebrations are called for. Remember this: each project, challenge, opportunity, or goal may be its own unique collaboration. A member who is a constructive critic, perfectionist, or introvert may be expected to generally rank your project lower than an optimist, "team player," or extrovert. The assessment is not to encourage the team to agree on the rankings; rather, insights are generated with respect to differences, trends, weaknesses, and strengths of the team, project, or collaboration. Like the Nine Domains,[26] leaders are to evaluate and tend to the health of the group to work better together. The assessment is not to weed out those that differ. Those that differ are often a team's strength.

Using the assessment as you start a collaboration as well as once you complete it are equally important. When you start a collaboration, the assessment may serve as a checklist to complement the 10 Steps in this book. The goal is to continuously focus on and improve the culture of collaboration in your organization.

These assessments may be charted over time by a team, an organization, and a collective that extends far outside your organizations boundaries. Revise the assessment to best suit your collaborative.

Looking at the results of the assessment:

- What becomes more evident?
- Where are the gaps?
- Can you identify your team's blind spots?
- Do you notice common themes?
- Are there wide discrepancies between the rankings of individual team members on any given question or group of questions?
- What do the results inform you about your organization's ecosystem?

Are the leaders working constantly to provide the mechanisms, alignments, and resources required? Can we truly hear, let go of judgments and expectations, and see possibilities greater than our own? These are some of the questions you may choose to consider quarterly and annually to assess your progress overall in building success. This assessment of the collaborative culture in your organization is most useful when done repeatedly over time and reviewed collaboratively. The transparent and constructive review of the assessment with your team will further the collaborative nature, openness, trust, and engagement of your team. Thanks to SVI 360, Laura Hummelle, and others for assisting me in creating this and the more detailed 360 Collaborative Leadership and Team Development Assessment.

Your Examples and Decisions

In the introduction, I mentioned issues that engaged me included:

- How to successfully advance economic development while protecting the environment and advancing the interest of the community
- How to evolve the energy transition conversation locally and globally
- How to identify, select, teach, and develop next generation leaders and board members
- How to save a project that has suffered from constantly changing requirements, costs, and designs
- How to create a regional non-motorized trails alliance
- How to decide on which initiative to champion when there are several attractive ones

Everyone of these are challenging and demand purposeful design. I am connecting people and resources and serving as a gathering place for generative conversation of what we wish to create together. And on most of these, I find it takes years to create the space and the vision. Then once the gatekeepers start to experience the energy and the results, they will participate fully. Be persistent. It is rarely easy. It is always worth it. Be the change. Be relentless for our better future.

What are your examples of initiatives that you wish to produce better outcomes?

1.

2.

3.

Before you decide, consider creating a decision matrix on your potential project. A decision matrix is a list of values in rows and columns that allows an analyst to systematically identify, analyze, and rate the performance of relationships between sets of values and information. Elements of a decision matrix show decisions based on certain decision criteria. The matrix is useful for looking at large masses of decision factors and assessing each factor's relative significance.[27]

Here is a sample based on How to Create a Regional Non-Motorized Trail Alliance.

Create your own based on your criteria.

Value criteria on a scale of 1 (no positive impact) to 5 (high positive impact).

CRITERIA	DO NOTHING	JUST LOCAL	REGIONAL
Marketing			
Funding			
Planning			
Sustainability			
Collaborative Intelligence			
Reducing Conflict			
Political Influence			
Serving Community			
Engagement			
Ongoing management demands			
Skills development			
Total			
Rank			
Status			

For your design, here is a blank template.

CRITERIA	A	B	C

A Call to Action

I challenge you to:

1. Actively use this Collaboration Guide in every new initiative

2. Customize the resources and templates in this guide to better suit your needs

3. Reach out to build your new global network of collaborators to help you decide, resource, and lead your initiatives, and

4. Report to me so that we will continually improve our processes, templates, and leadership. **david@davidbsavage.com**

Appendices

ADVICE FROM MY NETWORK

Trae Ashlie-Garen, 6 Acts of Receiving and The WINfinity Framework

1) Why is collaboration important to you?

We are entering an age where we are becoming more present to ourselves and each other, and we are learning what embodiment of the higher aspects of being human looks like. The intention toward collaboration is a pathway through our humanity, which guides all of us as integrated leaders, to step further into stewardship, and even into guardianship. The planet and the well-being of all living things on it are demanding that we all hold space for that learning journey and enter into the Aspiration of Collaboration.

2) Where do leaders fail as collaborators?

We prematurely narrow our solutions to be about resources—tools, processes, and environments—before we have fully allowed a space of inquiry to discover the common Core Values that are driving our actions, our thoughts, and ultimately our beliefs. At its core, our capacity to release any preconceived notions about "what it's going to take" (i.e. what is known), and allow ourselves to play in the unknown, is foundational to what is going to make or break how any gathering of people in the name of Collaboration, is ultimately going to go.

3) What is one thing you wish leaders would do more often to move their organizations forward?

I would encourage all of us to raise the narrative. Collaboration is not just a context-specific tool, or "best-practice-process," or even an environment. It is an Aspiration. We need to stop limiting collaboration to "applied convening" in the name of organizational branding or agenda, and entertain the idea that the movement toward Collaboration is, in its highest form, a Learning Context and a Learning Experience. Moving our focus toward a shared culture of "being in practice" by consciously entering into designed experiences which reach across silos of thought, and which expand our bandwidth for experimentation, and the experience of dealing with the unknown with whole (head and heart) intelligence, IS the next frontier.

4) When you are deciding on a new project, what resources, books, or people to you look to?

Otto Scharmer — The Presencing Institute

John Hagel — Deloitte's Centre for the Edge

Salim Ismail — Ongoing evolution of the ExO Sprint

Kathy Porter, President, The Collaborative Global Initiative and author of *Beyond Climate Shock: A Passionate Approach to Saving Community Without Draining the Bank*

1) Why is collaboration important to you?

Working together collaboratively can be both exciting and daunting. Relational beings, we are attracted to like-minded others. Humans have survived and evolved in part because we can work together. Driven by our amygdala or lizard brain, our fear of the unknown or difference can limit our ability to work together.

With humility, I have come to understand that our strength is in our difference. From nature, I recognize that in our diversity we are stronger. For ourselves and for our children, we can take small steps not only to survive but to thrive.

2) Where do leaders fail as collaborators?

There is a lack of interest, often driven by financial constraints, to bring in the appropriate third-party neutrals who have the skill to build collaborative partnerships and can stand outside of the project. This crucial step reduces the perspective that there is an inherent bias in the person leading the project towards an existing decision. The ability to reflect on the moral or ethical considerations is often lost in the rush towards solving a problem. With the solution a foregone conclusion, the evidence, scientific or otherwise, tends towards support. Flooding could be prevented by building canals, traffic snarls would be mitigated by building larger roads, or public opposition could be quieted by scientific evidence.

3) What is one thing you wish leaders would do more often to move their organizations forward?

Enable reflective and in-depth conversations where the employee does not risk loss of job or position as a result of honest feedback.

4) When you are deciding on a new project, what resources, books, or people to you look to?

I look to my close colleagues and friends, library books and journals, and then Google to search for other resources or connections.

Suzanne Sherkin, Q.Med, Highborn Communications Ontario, Canada

Where do leaders fail as collaborators?

Leaders by nature are strong minded, strong willed, and driven thinkers. These are great behaviours for driving towards a goal and getting it accomplished. If, as a team member, the vision makes sense to you—great. You'll be a cheerleader and enjoy the journey. However, if the vision isn't compatible with your own, you end up towing the line and just showing up to "get 'er done." As long as things get done, the leader likely won't notice or maybe even care about people's level of engagement. Outcome is key.

Herein lies the failing. Outcome is important, but engagement is the key. It's not enough for team members to be (passive) cooperators; for a team to be dynamic, creative, and engaged, people need to be (active) collaborators. That could mean challenging the leader's view and asking time-consuming and possibly uncomfortable questions. It seems to me that leaders can present themselves as collaborative—so long as everyone on the team supports their vision. What they're really wanting is helpful agreement. The failing: mistaking cooperation for collaboration.

Jeffrey M. Cohen, Esq., Mediator, New York, USA

1) Why is collaboration important to you?

Collaboration is a foundational strategy in my mediation model. Rather than focus on the dispute that brings the parties to the mediation table, I first focus on helping the parties achieve understanding and trust. Once both parties have established trust and understanding, they will more readily collaborate to resolve the issues at hand.

2) Where do leaders fail as collaborators?

Leaders fail by clinging to an archaic, "top down" leadership style where they make decisions and expect those below to simply engage in implementation strategies. This approach creates an atmosphere where employees do not feel that they have a stake in the organization and where employees do not feel that they are important participants in its overall success. This approach dampens an employee's morale, motivation, and creativity. As a result, growth and productivity suffer.

3) What is one thing you wish leaders would do more often to move their organizations forward?

The better leadership mode is to adopt a collaborative and participatory strategy that engages employees in team building, decision-making, and the creation of innovative outcomes. This approach gives employees a stake in the outcome of the organization and fosters a creative, innovative, and cohesive working atmosphere.

4) When you are deciding on a new project, what resources, books, or people to you look to?

I seek out the wisdom of my peers.

Sara *(age 8)* and Quinn *(age 10)* Amos, British Columbia, Canada

We collaborate to make friends and do better work.

Jeanne S. McPherson, PhD, Washington State, USA

As Rotary increasingly reaches across the generations—from Interact to Rotaract, through Gen Xs, Boomers and beyond—clubs can find themselves challenged by values and ideas new and often uncomfortable, especially to those who want to keep their clubs "the same." Our work orientation and ethics—which we all bring to Rotary—are shaped not only by our peer groupings, but also by our families, religious training, fields of study, cultures of origin, gender, and other influences unique to our particular life experiences.

Knowing generational trends may offer a context to help us understand certain behaviours we observe, it's still the relational issues that matter the most for successful clubs and project outcomes.

No matter what our age, most of us want to have a voice in club decisions, share our ideas, and be appreciated for our contributions. We want opportunities to do meaningful work, expanding our reach as we grow in our expertise. In disagreements, we want our ideas considered respectfully.

Generational distinctions highlight a need to reclaim the basics: skills in listening, communication, relationship-building, decision-making, teamwork, and conflict management. Collaborative interaction skills can help club members side-step tensions and spur creative action spanning all generations.

Marie-Jose Caire, Rotary Friendship Exchange, Chair and Secrétaire District 1700, Toulouse, France

1) Why is collaboration important to you?

Alone we go faster, but together we go further!

2) Where do leaders fail as collaborators?

Due to a lack of a medium or long term vision!

3) What is one thing you wish leaders would do more often to move their organizations forward?

Get involved personally and meet members individually to listen carefully to their request. Choose correct members to give recognition and be more objective.

4) When you are deciding on a new project, what resources, books, or people to you look to?

As far as Rotary is concerned, we are lucky to have a lot of information on the web site, and if we look carefully we can have all the answers to our questions.

THE ROTARY SURVEY

The Survey

During March 2018, I composed a ten-question online survey to obtain perspectives from active Rotarians globally. The survey was titled, "How Will We Improve Rotary Collaborations with Stakeholders and Members." The survey received 40 complete responses and included participation from a District Governor, a new Rotarian E-Club members, and Rotarians from Canada, America, and France. This survey is indicative but not scientifically accurate.

What We Learned

Here are a few of the results:

*Question: **What are examples of collaborations you think Rotary can do far better at?***

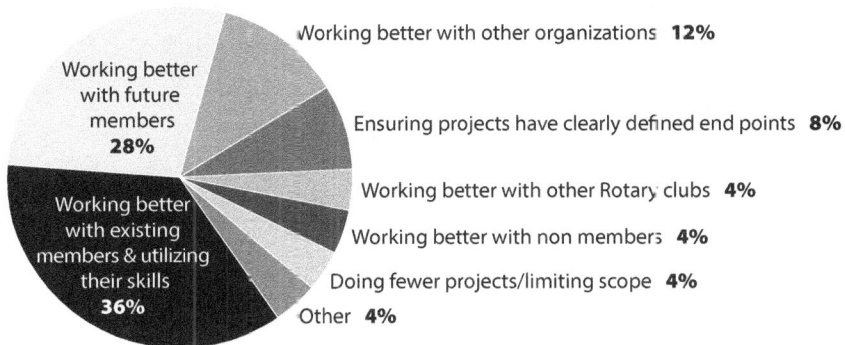

*Question: **What is an example of a poorly designed collaboration and what should be done better?***

A sample of responses:

"I was attracted to Rotary as they have immense power globally in the multiplication of manpower and finance. However, it seems to me that many in the Rotary act "as their own boss" and this may be fine as it creates a free-market and entrepreneurial environment for getting projects started. There appears to be resistance to change from some members, and this may not allow for changes that may need to happen to adopt the next generation of Rotarians—and I think this needs to be a priority.

"Any project designed and pursued in a vacuum. Often small, passionate groups of people band together and charge ahead, but the balance of the club could be left behind. The problem is always the passionate few doing the heavy lifting, but finding a key to keep all engaged would be beneficial.

"Our District Leadership team is comprised of the District Board (10), Assistant Governors (13), and District Committees (5) which tend to operate in silos and not together as a collaborative team."

Question: Speaking from your experience in Rotary, where are we most challenged in meeting our objectives?

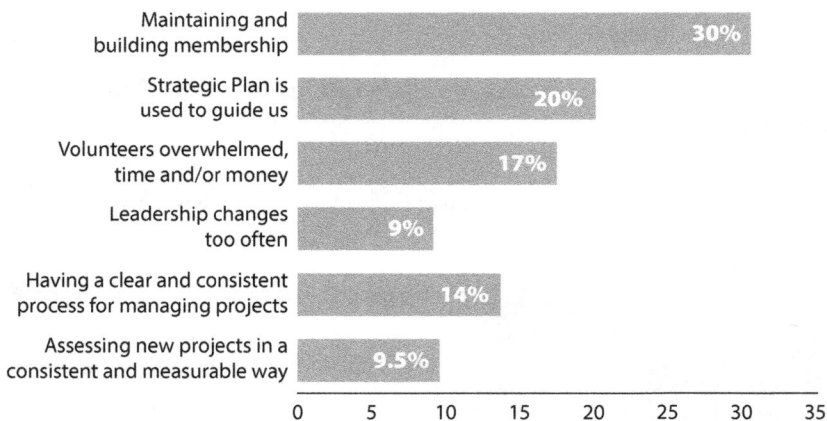

Category	Value
Maintaining and building membership	30%
Strategic Plan is used to guide us	20%
Volunteers overwhelmed, time and/or money	17%
Leadership changes too often	9%
Having a clear and consistent process for managing projects	14%
Assessing new projects in a consistent and measurable way	9.5%

This was a matrix ranking question. These are the #1 choices only.

Question: What are the main characteristics of a well-designed collaboration?

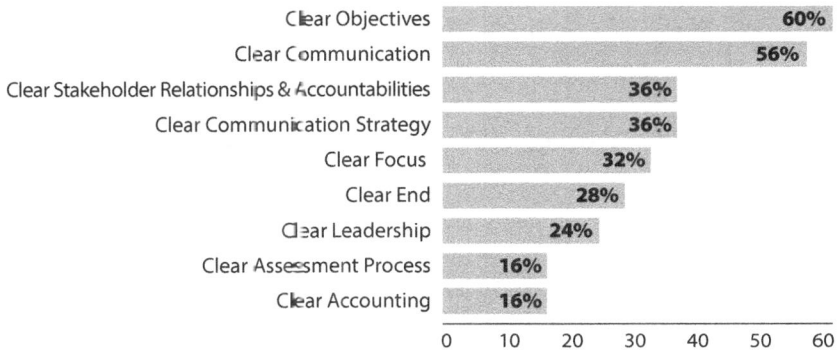

Characteristic	Percentage
Clear Objectives	60%
Clear Communication	56%
Clear Stakeholder Relationships & Accountabilities	36%
Clear Communication Strategy	36%
Clear Focus	32%
Clear End	28%
Clear Leadership	24%
Clear Assessment Process	16%
Clear Accounting	16%

Question: Do you believe you have access to a concise, useful guide through Rotary to help you collaborate?

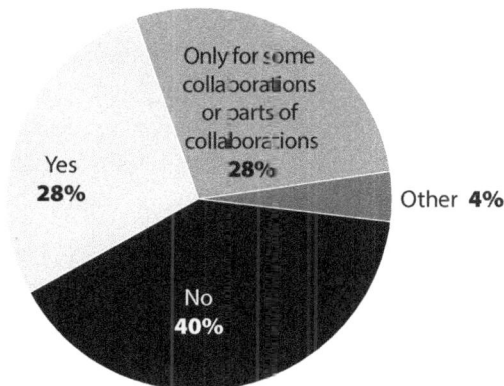

Only for some collaborations or parts of collaborations 28%

Yes 28%

Other 4%

No 40%

From these March 2018 survey results, it appears that this guide book is a needed resource While my survey focused on 40 Rotary International leaders, we may find similar results for many organizations. Organizations, multinational and start-ups, may have websites, procedure manuals and other resources to help leaders. Unfortunately, few have a concise guide and many of a variety of places you must find.

ANOTHER LOOK AT THE
10 ESSENTIAL STEPS

Step 1 — Set Intention, declare your honest purpose. One of the key questions now is "how comfortable are you with not knowing the outcome?" Few leaders are—they've got their objective, their goal, their target, their budget. I hope your intention is to collaborate in all its beauty, in all its challenges for whatever the collective wisdom brings to the group. It's Break Through to a greater Yes. Focus on intention not outcome.

Step 2—Be Aware, engage others with an open heart. Often, you'll realize that people in your organization, your community, or your family don't have the same drive, the same motivation, the same interest as you. Often, they're just watching—they're not really engaged. Understand what their alternatives are. Understand what they'd prefer. Are they monitoring and maybe blocking? ... gathering information? ...or are they fully in?

Step 3—Embrace Conflict. If they're blocking, that moves us to seek out those that speak out. Don't get sucked into *yes man group think*. When people speak out and push back on me, that's a gift. There's something very important to them that they think I'm not respecting. They give me the opportunity to learn. They give me an opportunity to include for the greater outcome. Give them a voice.

Step 4—Seek Diversity, bring in many perspectives. Young, old, black, white, whatever culture. Bring in the women. Bring in the elders. Bring in the Serbians. Bring in the Inuit. Bring in the Piikani. Whoever those people are that will be affected by your collaboration, bring them in. It's like having a constructive critic. It's like having somebody that doesn't see the way I see. They are a gift bearing new perspectives. And if you deny them here, they will show up later, and that will not be productive.

Step 5 — Design the Collaboration, imagine success and create the right container. Who are the right people, what is the right time, the right place, the right resources, the right intentions? Even the physical design, architects, and interior designers design spaces based on how we create a space that creates innovation, creativity. Think about going outside. Think about having your collaboration under a tree, under a 1,000-year-old tree, around a campfire. Think about sitting in that field that's going to be affected, connecting to the earth. Yeah, it's not that hard, but it's not that common.

Step 6—Come Together. Come together, meet, engage with respect and trust.

Step 7—Listen Deeply, realize what wants to be heard but is not spoken. In my coaching certification, we reviewed three levels of listening. The first level is listening to the words of the person who's speaking to you. The second level is what is underneath the person's words. The third level is listening to the energy in the room—the energy of the collective. Is there something here in this room that isn't being spoken that wants to be spoken?

Step 8—Collaborate with Vision, tap into the collective wisdom. Yeah, the collective wisdom. This often starts from: where do we want to be together five years from now, ten years from now? What's our future desired state for our organization, for our company, for our community? Whatever that is, what is our future desired state? Based on your values, based on the principles, based on the resources available, the challenges and opportunities in your organizations or community, those need to be understood, explored, in order to find a vision. Is it a vision that makes your team, your organization and our world a better place? Does your vision serve social good? Or is it something that you as leader can agree with—the environmentalist, the youth, the chamber of commerce, the politicians? Is it something that you can agree on together? This is where we're going, this is where we want to be, and this is how we will all collaborate.

Step 9—Now Lead, with purpose and accountability. Now, this comes to the traditional leadership. Often people will collaborate when they don't want to lead. Death by consultation, death by collaboration. No, it's both. For the first eight steps, you as leader are holding the space, creating the container, building the power, the culture, the innovation, the creativity, the "but." Even saying that, I can feel it. Now lead. Let's talk about purpose, let's talk about measurables and accountability. Time to step into that leadership role. You are the driver.

Step 10—Make It So, positively change the energy and the future together. Continual collaboration, continual evolution, learning together. Continual 10 steps, keep going, keep going, keep going.

I believe that many possibilities are left unseen, untapped, unclaimed. Together we are better. Together we can do a far better job. So, let's get out there and collaborate more effectively to produce better outcomes.[28]

MORE WISDOM

Moving Beyond the Generational Divide
by Jeanne McPherson, Washington, USA [29]

We are all more than our generational labels. Our work orientation and ethics are shaped not only our peer groupings, but also by our families, religious training, fields of study, cultures of origin, gender, and other influences unique to our particular life experiences.

Knowing generational trends may offer a context in which to explore certain behaviors we observe; yet, it's still the relational issues that matter the most for successful teams and organizational outcomes.

No matter what our age, most of us want to have a voice in decisions that affect us, share our ideas, and be appreciated for our contributions. We want opportunities to do meaningful work, expanding our reach as we grow in our expertise. In disagreements, we want our ideas considered respectfully. Such workplace conditions go beyond labels that divide us.

We might agree that generational distinctions highlight a need to reclaim the basics: skills in listening, communication, relationship-building, decision-making, teamwork, and conflict management. Intergenerational development emphasizing collaborative interaction skills can go a long way toward moving us beyond the generational divide.

Measuring Trust
by Donna Kennedy-Glans, author of *Corporate Integrity: A Toolkit for Managing Beyond Compliance and Beyond Complexity,* Alberta, Canada [30]

One of the ultimate goals of engagement is building trust. How do you know when you have succeeded? A simple question, but not easily answered. It's easier to talk about trust than it is to do trust-building… and, it's easier to do trust-building than it is to measure trust.

You know what it feels like when you don't have trust in relationships with others: the churning, the cynicism, the shrugs and indifference. You also know what it feels like to trust and be trusted. Beyond gut feel, how do you measure rising and ebbing levels of trust as an organization?

"A single conversation stifled by a lack of trust doesn't seem that significant but multiply such a conversation thousands or millions of times, and the macro effects can be profound," says innovation guru, Victor Hwang.[31]

To measure the outcomes of your trust-building efforts, your organization must figure out how to account for the millions of invisible, intangible interactions. This microscopic approach is daunting! We do have the economic tools needed to capture the value of fiscal measures. But we don't, yet, have the economic tools to capture the value of these relationships.

Many corporate valuators I talk to see a correlation between these beyond-financial measures and corporate performance. Positive differentiation of your organization is possible, but only if you can credibly measure and report on these beyond-financial indicators.

What we need to do is more intentionally measure trust. We need new tools. And thankfully, there are really smart people thinking about this challenge.

Sarah Thorne describes trust as a measurable outcome:

"In our work, trust is an outcome—a critical component of citizen or stakeholder judgment. There are many factors that influence public judgment of the acceptability of something, say a proposed energy project—and the weighting of those factors varies from community to community."[32]

For people like Sarah, trust is recognized as an essential underpinning of working relationships, measurable by actions or behaviors.

In innovation space, people like Victor Hwang are building measurement models that allow entrepreneurs to measure the rhythms or waves of trust in their ocean of extended networks...without having to measure the dynamics of every single wave. It's impossible to monitor the trust in every relationship, between every node, but it's not impossible to measure the waves, or flow, of trust moving through an organization and its wider network.

So how do you start to measure trust? Begin by setting your own trust indicators. *In your organization, what are you looking for, beyond gut feel...what are the signs of positive trust with targeted stakeholders?*

Keep your fingers on the pulse of your organization.

Here are some practical ideas of trust indicators that have worked for others:

- How do you make decisions?
- Are you transparent about how decisions are made, and who is the decision-maker?
- What decisions is your organization positioned to share with others? What actual decisions does your organization share with others?
- How are diverse points of view invited into conversations and decision-making?
- Do you engage across worldviews (e.g. 'my way' people participating in your organization's idea, or vice versa; outreach to 'our way' citizens in advance of policy decisions by 'the way' decision-makers)?
- How do you deal with dissenting opinions? Do you share dissenting opinions? In the judicial system, dissenting views of justices are written up as part of the judgement and are recognized as having value.
- What about the timing of your engagement with others...do you reach out to others early enough in the decision-making or consultation process?

How do you communicate and report?

- Do you create physical or electronic stakeholder engagement maps? How do you share these maps?
- Do you reflect local or community knowledge in decision-making?
- How is the language of fairness and equity and values included in your engagement process and communications (e.g. not just scientific, technical, legal, engineering, and risking language)?
- Have you considered Integrated Reporting—a narrative report, supported by traditional financial reports, reflecting trust-building with others as one of many factors material to your value creation?
- How transparently do you share information about decisions made (e.g. apportionment of costs and benefits, scientific and technical assessment of risks, timelines, responsibility for decision-making, influence of stakeholders)?

Do you continuously improve your engagement processes?

- Do you update your engagement approaches (e.g. nudging surveys replaced with face-to-face meetings supplemented with ongoing, online mental modelling)?
- How often do you create unconventional venues for engagement? (e.g. move from head office to local communities, on-line, more public space)

- When do you use third-party facilitators to host dialogues?
- Do you conduct post-project audits of engagement strategies with key stakeholders to identify what's working and what's not working?

What are you measuring?

- The pace of funding of public-private partnerships?
- Reductions in the time-frames needed to gain regulatory approvals for new projects?
- Changes in the number of legal interventions or legal causes of action disrupting your operations?
- Reductions in complaints from communities regarding a new project?
- Improvements in competitive advantage and market share vis-à-vis your competitors (e.g preferential access to a project, partner of choice, and supply chain with capacity to navigate a new market risk)?
- Changes in your organization's reputation?
- Improvements in employee attraction and retention? (And what do you do with employees who have proven to be untrustworthy?)

You can change the conversation about trust.

Rather than waiting until you have a crisis of trust in your organization— the disaster that stops you in your tracks—keep your fingers on the pulse of your organization.

Beyond gut feel, set indicators to monitor trust. Know when your trust levels are rising or falling, and why. When you lower the barriers for distrust in a system, it's like opening up the arteries in your organization. It's a healthy pulse.

"Google Spent Years Studying Effective Teams. This Single Quality Contributed Most to Their Success"
by Justin Bariso, New York, USA[33]

The researchers found that what really mattered was less about who is on the team, and more about how the team worked together.

What mattered most: Trust.

So what was the most important factor contributing to a team's effectiveness? It was psychological safety. Simply put, psychological safety refers to an individual's perception of taking a risk, and the response his or her teammates will have to taking that risk.

Google describes it this way: In a team with high psychological safety, teammates feel safe to take risks around their team members. They feel confident that no one on the team will embarrass or punish anyone else for admitting a mistake, asking a question, or offering a new idea. In other words, great teams thrive on trust.

This may appear to be a simple concept but building trust between team members is no easy task. For example, a team of just five persons brings along varying viewpoints, working styles, and ideas about how to get a job done.

Convening and Technology

"In an age of complexity, when partnerships are increasingly necessary to address or resolve difficult issues, the ability to convene takes on a renewed importance. This book is a practical guide for individuals and organizations seeking to develop or enhance their capacities to convene. Whether bringing together a group of colleagues to better understand a complicated matter, or assembling diverse stakeholders to develop mutual respect, convening can provide the most effective means for resolving problems. The process helps to build trust and chart a path forward." *David Mitchell, Calgary Chamber of Volunteer Organizations*[34]

"One way to encapsulate the leadership required to create an alternative future is to consider the leader as primarily a convener—not leader as special person, but leader as a citizen, sometimes with legitimate power, willing to do those things that can initiate something new in the world. In this way, "leader" belongs right up there with cook, carpenter, artist, and landscape designer. All of us can develop this ability with a small amount of teaching and an agreement to practice—the ultimate do-it-yourself movement." *Peter Block*[35]

As technology evolves, we must take advantage of the opportunities to connect with the resources we have at our disposal locally and globally. Virtual meeting technology such as Zoom, GoToMeeting, Skype, and others connect us at any time in any time zone. With an estimated 4,000,000,000 people around the planet connected to the internet now, we have access to resources and people like never before. In addition, recent developments in convening theory and in innovation provide us real drivers to connection and innovation.

Consider one example of a powerful and relatively recent technology by Richard Schultz of Wisdom Ways.

"Open Space Technology (OST) is a transformative meeting process that helps organizations or communities self-organize to solve complex problems or take advantage of emerging opportunities. This simple, efficient and effective process creates an open, collaborative environment for breakthroughs in innovation, problem solving, creativity, and productivity. An Open Space meeting taps into the passion, wisdom and knowledge of people and teams like no other group process can. It can be used in groups from 5 to 1000+ participants."[36]

Scenario Planning

In my 10 Essential Steps, Step 2 is Be Aware.

Barry Wilson, of CE Analytics, a cumulative effects expert, encourages us to do proper Scenario Planning the must include all five factors:

- ✓ Business
- ✓ Technical
- ✓ Social
- ✓ Environmental
- ✓ Political

"If we omit one or more of these as we assess, decide, design, and manage our projects, we may be blindsided—and our projects will fail.

Have you ever spent a whole bunch of time making a plan, and maybe not only a bunch of time, but a bunch of money putting together a very comprehensive plan for something that you want to do? And you've tried to do your due diligence. You tried to cover all the bases and meet all the requirements—you feel like you thought about everybody's perspective in putting together your plan. After a good long time and a fair bit of effort, your plan is finally done. Then you go out and share it with a bunch of other people you think will be interested. In my experience, doing that results in one of two different responses: either it's total silence, and I mean like crickets... and nobody even wants to hear you; or worse, you get a bit of a backlash, or maybe some resistance, or maybe even anger. Why does that happen? You know you've covered all the bases, you've met all the legal requirements, you try to do things with the best intent—but it's not well received.

Here's what I learned about that.

It is way better to bring people that my plan is going to influence or affect into the planning process early—right at the very beginning. That's a collaborative approach rather than a selling approach. And it has been my experience that the rewards of taking a collaborative approach—whether you're trying to organize something within your family or within your business or in a major project development—it is way better to have everybody engage with you at the beginning and collaborate. I talk a lot about this because we run into conflict a lot in land use planning by simply not engaging with others early enough in the process."[37]

Another expert in Scenario Planning is Greg MacGillivray of Scenarios2Strategy.

"The Challenge of Uncertainty: How do you make strategic decisions? How do you decide where to place your bets? Toyota has bet on hybrids; GM has bet on fuel cells. Shell bet on offshore and LNG in the 1970s. Those turned out to be great bets. BP placed a big bet on Russia. Nexen-Opti have bet on coke-to-gas technology. EnCana bet on North American gas; Talisman bet on global conventional oil and gas. All of these choices involve significant strategic risk—the risk associated with major investment decisions that involve long time frames and uncertain outcomes. These are big, tough decisions because they are often company-transforming. Think of a $10 billion investment in oil sands—it can take years to learn whether the decision is brilliant or a bust. Most difficult, the key factors influencing success are uncertain and beyond the control of the company. Such factors cannot be analyzed away. No amount of research can resolve risks rising from political, technological, environmental, or other factors. Expectations about the future that determine the consequences of strategic decisions cannot be reduced to a single forecast with any credibility or confidence. One approach to this dilemma is scenario planning. Scenarios are alternative descriptions of the future. They embrace uncertainty. Instead of trying to reduce uncertainty to a single most-likely forecast, scenarios try to identify the major forces driving change and the key uncertainties that lead to a wide range of possible future outcomes. Scenarios map out the boundaries of our uncertainties and provide a context of expectations for generating and evaluating strategic options. This process surfaces strategic risks, and opens thinking on new ways of managing or mitigating risk in implementing major strategies. While hard decisions are not removed and risks are not eliminated, decisions are based on a broader understanding of the risks and rewards. That is the task of senior management. The worst decision is one made in ignorance where the risks were knowable but were not identified or fully considered."[38]

Planning and Organizing
Rotary International[39]

"Well-planned service projects are more likely to have a strong impact and create effective and transparent communication between your community and club. Every community has its own unique assets and concerns. Many districts maintain networks of local experts (district resource network) with technical and project-planning expertise. Your district or regional experts can serve as advisors to help your club:

- Align a project with Rotary's areas of focus
- Obtain assistance with project design/planning and implementation
- Learn about the global grant process
- Conduct a community assessment
- Identify international partners
- Secure funding
- Ensure the sustainability of the project
- Establish measurement and evaluation benchmarks"

Links to More Resources

Ken Cloke
https://www.kencloke.com/

Donna Kennedy-Glans
https://www.linkedin.com/in/dkennedyglans/

Greg MacGillivray, Scenarios2Strategy
http://scenarios2strategy.com/docs/planning.html

Jeanne McPherson
http://mcpherson-wfdev.com/

David Mitchell, Art of Convening
http://davidjmitchell.ca/

Richard Schultz
http://www.wisdomways.net/

Barry Wilson, CE Analytics
https://www.barryjwilson.com/

Rotary Leadership Tools
http://rlifiles.com/files/en/

Rotary International Project Guidelines
https://my.rotary.org/en/take-action/develop-projects

Rotary Lifecycle of a Service Project videos
https://vimeo.com/75356768

Acknowledgements

In creating this book, I wish to acknowledge the contributions of my friends and collaborators including;

Richard Schultz, Wisdom Ways, **http://www.wisdomways.net/**

Maggie Powell, Maggie Powell Designs, **https://maggiepowelldesigns.com/**

And the forty Rotary International leaders from America, Canada and France that participated in the survey and in discussions on this guide.

Endnotes

1. https://www.theverge.com/2014/6/12/5804122/tesla-opens-patents-to-all

2. Victor Hwang Kauffman Foundation **https://www.kauffman.org/who-we-are/ leadership-and-associates/associates/victor-w-hwang**

3. Values and Ethics definition **https://www.reference.com/world-view/ ethics-important-6d182213bbb36d04?qo=contentSimilarQuestions#**

4. *Don't Think of an Elephant: Know Your Values and Frame the Debate*, George Lakoff **https://georgelakoff.com/2014/08/18/new-book-the-all-new-dont-think-of-an-elephant-know-your-values-and-frame-the-debate/**

5. Ken Cloke, **https://www.kencloke.com/**

6. *The Rainforest Book*, **http://www.therainforestbook.com/**

7. *Break Through To Yes: Unlocking the Possible within a Culture of Collaboration*, David B. Savage, **http://www.davidbsavage.com/books/**

8. https://www.snopes.com/news/2016/03/25/the-saga-of-twitter-bot-tay/

9. *Break Through To Yes: Unlocking the Possible within a Culture of Collaboration*, David B. Savage, **http://www.davidbsavage.com/books/**

10. *Start with Why*, Simon Sinek, **https://startwithwhy.com/**

11. Barry Wilson, **https://barryjwilson.com/**

12. Integrative Project Delivery **https://www.aiacontracts.org/resources/64146-integrated-project-delivery-a-guide**

13. Henry Ford (quote), **https://www.goodreads.com/quotes/118854-coming-together-is-the-beginning-keeping-together-is-progress-working**

14. Margaret Wheatly, http://margaretwheatley.com/

15. *Centered Leadership: Leading with Purpose, Clarity, and Impact*, McKinsey **https://www.mckinsey.com/business-functions/organization/our-insights/ centered-leadership**

16. Margaret Wheatly, **http://margaretwheatley.com/home/**

17. The Foundations for Collaboration, **https://www.amazon.com/Foundations-Collaboration-Break-Through-Collaborative/dp/1775130975/ref=sr_1_3?ie=UTF8&qi d=1525733508&sr=8-3&keywords=The+Foundations+for+Collaboration**

18. Forbes on Collaboration, Forbes.com, **http://www.forbes.com/sites/jwebb/2015/11/23/ why-supplier-collaboration-projects-keep-hitting-the-wall/**

19. *Break Through To Yes: Unlocking the Possible within a Culture of Collaboration*, David B. Savage **www.davidbsavage.com**

20. *The Purpose Effect*, Dan Pontefract, **http://www.danpontefract.com/ three-tough-questions-answered-about-purpose/**

21. C2CADR, **http://c2cadr.com/about/**

22. Diversity, *Forbes,* **https://www.forbes.com/sites/ekaterinawalter/2014/01/14/
reaping-the-benefits-of-diversity-for-modern-business-innovation/#590252582a8f**

23. https://www.stephen-covey.com/7habits/7habits-habit7.php

24. *Break Through to Yes: Unlocking the Possible within a Culture of Collaboration,*
David B. Savage, **www.davidbsavage.com**

25. 360 Collaborative Leadership Assessment Tool,
http://www.davidbsavage.com/360-degree-assessments/

26. Nine Domains of Leadership, **http://www.ninedomains.com/**

27. Decision Matrix, **https://en.wikipedia.org/wiki/Decision_matrix**

28. The Foundations for Collaboration, **http://www.davidbsavage.com/books/**

29. *Moving Beyond the Generational Divide,* Jeanne McPherson,
https://www.linkedin.com/in/jeanne-s-mcpherson-phd-04b71519/

30. Donna Kennedy Glans, **https://www.linkedin.com/in/dkennedyglans/**

31. Victor Hwang, **https://www.kauffman.org/who-we-are/leadership-and-associates/
associates/victor-w-hwang**

32. Sarah Thorne, **http://cognitivesciencesystems.com/**

33. Trust, **https://www.inc.com/justin-bariso/google-spent-years-studying-effective-teams-
this-single-quality-contributed-most-to-their-success.html**

34. *Art of Convening,* David Mitchell, **http://davidjmitchell.ca/2017/11/01/the-art-of-convening/**

35. *Art of Convening,* Peter Block **https://www.bkconnection.com/books/title/
the-art-of-convening**

36. Open Space Technology, Richard Schultz, **http://www.wisdomways.net/wisdom/
OpenSpaceTechnologyTraining/index.cfm**

37. *Cumulative Effects,* Barry Wilson, **https://www.barryjwilson.com/blog/war-in-the-woods**

38. Scenarios2Strategy, Greg McGillivray, **http://scenarios2strategy.com/docs/planning.html**

39. Rotary International Service Projects, **https://my.rotary.org/en/take-action/
develop-projects/project-lifecycle-resources**

About the Author

David B. Savage, BA (Econ), PLand, CPCC
Collaboration, Business Development, and Negotiation Specialist
Savage Management Ltd. / Consultant, Author, Speaker, Collaborator
david@davidbsavage.com | 403-466-5577 | www.davidbsavage.com

David Savage works with leaders and organizations to advance their success through collaboration, negotiation, conflict resolution, and business development. David brings 42+ years expertise, experience and leadership in oil and gas, renewable energy, health care, entrepreneurship, stakeholder engagement and conflict management. Over a ten-year period, David and partners, collaborated to develop 5 companies and 4 not for profits. Since 2007, Savage Management has focused on build capacity, innovation and accountability in people and in and between organizations and communities.

David Savage's Publications

2003: Company to Company Dispute Resolution Council: *Let's Talk Handbook*
2011: *Think Sustain Ability: Sustain Magazine*
2012: *Ready Aim Excel: 52 Leadership Lessons*
2013 *Sustain Magazine*, second issue
2016: *Break Through to Yes: Unlocking the Possible within a Culture of Collaboration*
2017: The Collaborative Podcast Series (print, eBook and Audible) include 75 guests from eight nations:
    Book 1: The Foundations for Collaboration
    Book 2: The Collaborative Guest Podcasts
    Book 3: The 10 Essential Steps
    Book 4: Unlocking the Possible
2018: *Break Through to Yes: Unlocking the Possible within a Culture of Collaboration*, Updated and Revised edition
Better by Design: Your Best Collaboration Guide, Produce Better Outcomes with Well Designed Collaborations